little book of

Gin

Cocktails

hamlyn

An Hachette Livre UK Company
First published in 2000 by Hamlyn, a division of Octopus Publishing Group Limited,
2–4 Heron Quays, London E14 4JP
Copyright © 2000 Octopus Publishing Group Ltd

Distributed in the United States and Canada by Sterling Publishing Co., Inc.
387 Park Avenue South, New York, NY 10016-8810

British Library Cataloguing-in-Publication Data
A catalogue record for this book is available from the British Library

ISBN-13: 978-0-600-61772-3
ISBN-10: 0-600-61772-6

Printed in China

10 9 8 7 6 5 4 3 2 1

Notes for American readers

The measure that has been used in the recipes is based on
a bar jigger, which is 45 ml (1½ fl oz). If preferred, a different
volume can be used providing the proportions are kept
constant within a drink and suitable adjustments are made
to spoon measurements, where they occur.

Standard level spoon measurements are used in all recipes.
1 tablespoon = one 15 ml spoon
1 teaspoon = one 5 ml spoon
Imperial and metric measurements have been given in
some of the recipes. Use one set of measurements only and
not a mixture of both.

UK	US
caster sugar	granulated sugar
cocktail cherries	maraschino cherries
cocktail stick	toothpick
double cream	heavy cream
drinking chocolate	presweetened cocoa powder
icing sugar	confectioners' sugar
jug	pitcher
lemon rind	lemon peel or zest
single cream	light cream
soda water	club soda

Contents

CLASSICS 8

A dazzling collection of drinks, many of which date back to the 1920s, including some of the most exciting gin cocktails yet devised.

EXOTIC COCKTAILS 30

With fantastic ingredients, such as the sapphire-coloured blue Curaçao, these exotic combinations make a wonderful collection of gin spectaculars.

COOLERS AND FIZZERS 50

These long refreshing drinks, such as the Sea Breeze and the Morning Glory Fizz will cool and invigorate on a hot summer's evening.

HIGH SPIRITS 74

From the Knockout to the Earthquake, these are serious cocktails, so watch your step.

Introduction

Gin is a clear grain spirit, further distilled with a variety of herb and fruit flavourings – the botanicals – which has been produced commercially for over 400 years. Originally from Holland, it has had a chequered social career, sinking to the lowest social depths in 18th-century London, when it was distilled from anything that would ferment, before rising to a respected place among the mixed drinks of the Victorian age – the fizzes, fixes and slings – and the strong, potent mixes of the cocktail age of the 1920s.

Gins of previous centuries would not be to the taste of present-day drinkers, for they were strongly flavoured and very sweet. During the 19th century London gained a reputation for its dry gin, which was distilled from the pure water from villages on the edge of the countryside such as

Clerkenwell and Finsbury. London dry gin is now a generic term for unsweetened dry gin and, although it can be made anywhere in the world, some countries will only permit the description 'London dry' if the gin is imported from the United Kingdom. Plymouth gin, which can only be made in Plymouth, is a more aromatic, slightly sweetened gin. It has always been held in great affection by the Royal Navy, who have a tradition that true Pink Gin must be made with Plymouth gin. Dutch gin (which may be labelled Holland's or Geneva) has a fuller flavour still, while Sloe Gin (gin flavoured with sloes and sugar) is a bright clear red – delicious as an after-dinner drink.

The flavour of gin varies subtly from one brand to the next. It is also important when choosing a gin to look closely at the label. Some types are lower in alcohol than others (they range in percentage volume from 47.3 to 37.5%), resulting in a less potent drink. All alcoholic drinks contain congeners (the elements in alcohol that cause hangovers). There are fewer of these in colourless spirits such as vodka than in spirits like whisky and rum, and fewest of all in gin.

Gin makes an ideal base for cocktails because it blends well with other flavours, whets the appetite rather than dulling it and gives the drinker an instant lift. It is not for nothing that the most famous cocktail of all time – the Dry Martini – is a gin-based drink. Famous Dry Martini drinkers include Noel Coward, W C Fields, Dean Martin, Humphrey Bogart and Ernest Hemingway.

After the gin, ice is probably the most important ingredient in a cocktail. It has two functions, chilling the drink and acting as a beater in the shaker.

Crushed ice cools a drink more quickly than cracked ice, but dilutes it more rapidly. Always use tongs to transfer ice to glasses; using a spoon means that you risk adding water with the ice. When mixing drinks, clear drinks are normally stirred in a mixing glass, while cloudy drinks (those containing egg white, cream or fruit juices) are shaken in a blender or cocktail shaker and then strained, ideally into a chilled glass.

Sugar Syrup
This may be used instead of sugar to sweeten cocktails and to give them more body. It can be bought, but is simple to make at home.

Put 4 tablespoons of sugar and 4 tablespoons water in a small pan and stir over a low heat until the sugar has dissolved. Bring to the boil and boil, without stirring, for 1–2 minutes. Store in a sterilized bottle in the refrigerator for up to 2 months.

Classics

Dry Martini

New Orleans Dry Martini

Horse's Neck

Opera

Clover Club

Pink Clover Club

Albermarle Fizz

Bronx

White Lady

Maiden's Prayer

Monkey Gland

Paradise

French '75

Orange Blossom

Dry Martini

5–6 ice cubes
½ measure dry vermouth
3 measures gin
1 green olive

The Dry Martini, which was invented at the Knickerbocker Hotel in New York in 1910, has become the most famous cocktail of all. Lemon rind is sometimes used as a decoration instead of a green olive.

Put the ice cubes into a mixing glass. Pour the vermouth and gin over the ice and stir (never shake) vigorously and evenly without splashing, then strain into a chilled cocktail glass. Serve with a green olive.

Serves 1

New Orleans Dry Martini

5–6 ice cubes
2–3 drops pernod
1 measure dry vermouth
4 measures gin

Put the ice cubes into a mixing glass. Pour the pernod over the ice, then pour in the vermouth and gin. Stir (never shake) vigorously and evenly without splashing. Strain into a chilled cocktail glass.

Serves 1

Horse's Neck

4–6 ice cubes, cracked
1½ measures gin
dry ginger ale
long spiral of lemon rind

Put the ice into a tall glass and pour in the gin. Top up with dry ginger ale then dangle the lemon rind over the edge of the glass.

Serves 1

Variation

This classic cocktail can also be made with a brandy, rum or whisky base instead of gin. The spiral of lemon rind is essential.

13

Opera

4–5 ice cubes
1 measure Dubonnet
½ measure Curaçao
2 measures gin
orange rind spiral, to
    decorate

Put the ice cubes into a mixing glass. Pour the Dubonnet, Curaçao and gin over the ice. Stir evenly, then strain into a chilled cocktail glass. Decorate with the orange rind spiral and serve.

Serves 1

Clover Club

4–5 ice cubes
juice of 1 lime
½ teaspoon sugar syrup
    (see page 7)
1 egg white
3 measures gin

to decorate
grated lime rind
lime wedge

Put the ice cubes into a cocktail shaker. Pour the lime juice, sugar syrup, egg white and gin over the ice and shake until a frost forms. Strain into a tumbler and serve decorated with grated lime rind and a lime wedge.

Serves 1

Pink Clover Club

4–5 ice cubes
juice of 1 lime
dash of grenadine
1 egg white
3 measures gin
strawberry slice, to
    decorate

Grenadine is a sweet non-alcoholic syrup made from pomegranates, which give it its rich rosy pink colour.

Put the ice cubes into a cocktail shaker. Pour the lime juice, grenadine, egg white and gin over the ice. Shake until a frost forms, then strain into a cocktail glass. Decorate with a strawberry slice and serve with a straw.

Serves 1

Albemarle Fizz

4–6 ice cubes
1 measure gin
juice of ½ lemon
2 dashes raspberry syrup
½ teaspoon sugar syrup
    (see page 7)
soda water
cocktail cherries, to
    decorate

Put 2-3 ice cubes into a mixing glass and add the gin, lemon juice, raspberry syrup and sugar syrup. Stir to mix then strain into a highball glass. Add 2-3 fresh ice cubes and top up with soda water. Decorate with two cherries on a cocktail stick and serve with straws.

Serves 1

Bronx

cracked ice

1 measure gin

1 measure sweet
  vermouth

1 measure dry vermouth

2 measures fresh orange
  juice

Place some cracked ice, the gin,
sweet and dry vermouths and
orange juice in a cocktail shaker.
Shake to mix. Pour into a small
glass, straining the drink if
preferred.

Serves 1

White Lady

3–4 ice cubes
2 measures gin
1 measure Cointreau
1 teaspoon lemon juice
about ½ teaspoon egg
    white
spiral of lemon rind, to
    decorate

Place the ice cubes, gin, Cointreau, lemon juice and egg white in a cocktail shaker. Shake to mix then strain into a cocktail glass. Decorate with the spiral of lemon.

Serves 1

To make a Pink Lady, substitute 1 teaspoon grenadine for the Cointreau.

Maiden's Prayer

4–5 ice cubes
3 drops Angostura bitters
juice of 1 lemon
1 measure Cointreau
2 measures gin

Put the ice cubes into a cocktail shaker. Pour the bitters over the ice, add the lemon juice, Cointreau and gin and shake until a frost forms. Strain into a cocktail glass and serve with a straw.

Serves 1

Monkey Gland

1 measure orange juice
2 measures gin
3 dashes pernod
3 dashes grenadine
3–4 ice cubes

Put the orange juice, gin, pernod and grenadine into a cocktail shaker with 3-4 ice cubes. Shake well then strain into a chilled cocktail glass.

Serves 1

Paradise

2–3 ice cubes, cracked
1 measure gin
½ measure apricot brandy
½ measure fresh orange
    juice
dash of fresh lemon juice

to decorate
1 orange slice
1 lemon slice

Place the ice cubes in a cocktail shaker and add the gin, apricot brandy and orange and lemon juices. Shake to mix then strain into a cocktail glass. Decorate with the orange and lemon slices.

Serves 1

French '75

cracked ice
1 measure gin
juice of ½ lemon
1 teaspoon caster sugar
chilled Champagne or
    sparkling dry white
    wine
orange slice, to decorate

'It hits the spot with remarkable precision', wrote a cocktail book eighty years ago about the French '75. It still does!

Half fill a tall glass with cracked ice. Add the gin, lemon juice and sugar and stir well. Top up with chilled Champagne and serve with an orange slice.

Serves 1

Orange Blossom

1 measure gin
1 measure sweet
    vermouth
1 measure fresh orange
    juice
2–3 ice cubes
orange slices, to
    decorate

This is a cocktail from the prohibition years, when it was also sometimes known as an Adirondack. The orange juice could disguise a hearty slug of rotgut gin.

Pour the gin, vermouth and orange juice into a cocktail shaker and shake to mix. Place the ice cubes in a tumbler and strain the cocktail over them. Decorate the rim of the glass with orange slices.

Serves 1

Exotic Cocktails

Crossbow

4–5 ice cubes
½ measure gin
½ measure crème de
    cacao
½ measure Cointreau
drinking chocolate
    powder, to decorate

Put the ice cubes into a cocktail shaker and add the gin, crème de cacao and Cointreau. Dampen the rim of a chilled cocktail glass with a little water then dip the rim into a saucer of drinking chocolate. Shake the drink vigorously then strain into the prepared glass.

Serves 1

Gin Tropical

4–6 ice cubes
1½ measures gin
1 measure fresh lemon
    juice
1 measure passion fruit
    juice
½ measure fresh orange
    juice
soda water
orange rind spiral, to
    decorate

Put 2–3 ice cubes into a cocktail shaker, pour in the gin, lemon juice, passion fruit juice and orange juice and shake well. Put 2–3 fresh ice cubes into an old-fashioned glass and strain the cocktail over the ice. Top up with soda water and stir gently. Decorate with an orange rind spiral.

Serves 1

Long Island Iced Tea

8 ice cubes
½ measure gin
½ measure vodka
½ measure white rum
½ measure tequila
½ measure Cointreau
1 measure lemon juice
½ teaspoon sugar syrup
    (see page 7)
cola, to top up
lemon slice, to decorate

Put 2 ice cubes into a mixing glass. Add the gin, vodka, rum, tequila, Cointreau, lemon juice and sugar syrup. Stir well, then strain into a tall glass almost filled with the remaining ice cubes. Top up with cola and decorate with the slice of lemon.

Serves 1

Golden Dawn

4–5 ice cubes
juice of ½ orange
1 measure Calvados
1 measure apricot brandy
3 measures gin
soda water
skewered orange rind, to
    decorate

Put the ice cubes into a cocktail shaker. Pour the orange juice, Calvados, apricot brandy and gin over the ice and shake until a frost forms. Strain into a highball glass, top up with soda water and decorate with orange rind.

Serves 1

Juliana Blue

crushed ice
1 measure gin
½ measure Cointreau
½ measure blue Curaçao
2 measures pineapple
    juice
½ measure fresh lime
    juice
1 measure cream of
    coconut
1–2 ice cubes

to decorate
pineapple slice
cocktail cherries

Put some crushed ice into a blender and pour in the gin, Cointreau, blue Curaçao, pineapple and lime juices and cream of coconut. Blend at high speed for several seconds until the mixture has a consistency of soft snow. Put the ice cubes into a cocktail glass and strain the mixture on to them. Decorate with a pineapple slice and cocktail cherries. Serve with straws.

Serves 1

Cherry Julep

3–4 ice cubes
juice of ½ lemon
1 teaspoon sugar syrup
    (see page 7)
1 teaspoon grenadine
1 measure cherry brandy
1 measure sloe gin
2 measures gin
chopped ice
lemon rind strips, to
    decorate

Put the ice cubes into a cocktail shaker. Pour the lemon juice, sugar syrup, grenadine, cherry brandy, sloe gin and gin over the ice. Fill a highball glass with finely chopped ice. Shake the mixture until a frost forms then strain it into the ice-filled glass. Decorate with lemon rind strips and serve.

Serves 1

Bijou

3 ice cubes, cracked
1 measure gin
½ measure green
     Chartreuse
½ measure sweet
     vermouth
dash of orange bitters

to decorate
1 green olive
piece of lemon rind

Chartreuse is made by the Carthusian monks at their monastery near Grenoble, in the French Alps. The recipe is a secret but it is known to contain over 130 different herbs. There are two versions, green which is the stronger, and the weaker but sweeter yellow.

Put the ice cubes into a mixing glass and add the gin, Chartreuse, vermouth and bitters. Stir well and strain into a cocktail glass. Place the olive on a cocktail stick and add to the cocktail then squeeze the zest from the lemon rind over the surface.

Serves 1

Night of Passion

2 measures gin
1 measure Cointreau
1 tablespoon fresh lemon
   juice
2 measures peach nectar
2 tablespoons
   passionfruit juice
6–8 ice cubes

Put the gin, Cointreau, lemon juice, peach nectar and passionfruit juice into a cocktail shaker with 3–4 ice cubes and shake well. Strain into an old-fashioned glass over 3–4 fresh ice cubes.

Serves 1

Sapphire Martini

4 ice cubes
2 measures gin
½ measure blue Curaçao
1 red or blue cocktail
    cherry (optional)

Although blue Curaçao gives this drink its stunning colour, it is an orange flavoured liqueur.

Put the ice cubes into a cocktail shaker. Pour in the gin and blue Curaçao. Shake well to mix. Strain into a cocktail glass and carefully drop in a cocktail cherry, if using.

Serves 1

Peach Blow

8 cracked ice cubes
juice of ½ lemon or 1 lime
4 strawberries, crushed
1½ teaspoons caster
    sugar
1 tablespoon double
    cream
2 measures gin
soda water
strawberry slices, to
    decorate

**This recipe is deceptive.
Despite its name, it is
actually an alcoholic version
of strawberries and cream.**

Put 4 of the ice cubes into a
cocktail shaker, add the lemon
juice, strawberries, sugar, double
cream and gin and shake well.
Strain into a tall glass and top up
with soda water. Decorate with
strawberry slices.

Serves 1

Honolulu

4–5 ice cubes
1 measure pineapple
   juice
1 measure fresh lemon
   juice
1 measure fresh orange
   juice
½ teaspoon grenadine
3 measures gin

to decorate
pineapple slice
cocktail cherry

Put the ice cubes into a cocktail shaker. Pour the pineapple, lemon and orange juices, the grenadine and gin over the ice and shake until a frost forms. Strain the drink into a chilled cocktail glass and decorate with the pineapple and cherry.

Serves 1

Ben's Orange Cream

4–5 ice cubes
1 measure Cointreau
1 measure single cream
3 measures gin
1 tablespoon sugar syrup
    (see page 7)
chocolate flake, to
    decorate

Put the ice cubes into a cocktail shaker. Pour the Cointreau, cream and gin over the ice. Add the sugar syrup to the gin mixture and shake until a frost forms. Pour into a large glass and decorate with a chocolate flake.

Serves 1

Coolers & Fizzers

Gin Sling

Gin Cup

Gin Cooler

Gin Floradora

Sea Breeze

Morning Glory Fizz

Sydney Fizz

Gin Fix

Singapore Gin Sling

Salty Dog

Honeydew

John Collins

Lime Gin Fizz

Pink Gin

Gin Sling

4–5 ice cubes

juice of ½ lemon

1 measure cherry brandy

3 measures gin

soda water

cherries, to decorate
(optional)

Put the ice cubes into a cocktail shaker. Pour the lemon juice, cherry brandy and gin over the ice and shake until a frost forms. Pour without straining into a hurricane glass and top up with soda water. Decorate with cherries, if liked, and serve with straws.

Serves 1

Gin Cup

3 mint sprigs, extra to
  decorate
1 teaspoon sugar syrup
chopped ice
juice of ½ lemon
3 measures gin

Put the mint and sugar syrup into an old-fashioned glass and stir them about to bruise the mint slightly. Fill the glass with chopped ice, add the lemon juice and gin and stir until a frost begins to form. Decorate with extra mint sprigs.

Serves 1

Gin Cooler

3–4 ice cubes
½ teaspoon grenadine
juice of 1 lemon
3 measures gin
soda water

to decorate
1 cocktail cherry
1 lemon slice

Put the ice cubes into a highball glass. Pour the grenadine over the ice, then the lemon juice and the gin and stir evenly allowing the mixture to blend. Top up the drink with soda water. Decorate with a cocktail cherry and a lemon slice.

Serves 1

Gin Floradora

4–5 ice cubes
½ teaspoon sugar syrup
(see page 7)
juice of ½ lime
½ teaspoon grenadine
2 measures gin
dry ginger ale
twist of lime rind, to
decorate

Put the ice cubes into a cocktail shaker. Pour in the sugar syrup, lime juice, grenadine and gin and shake until a frost forms. Pour without straining into a hurricane glass. Top up with dry ginger ale, decorate with a lime twist and serve.

Serves 1

Sea Breeze

6–8 ice cubes
½ measure fresh
    grapefruit juice
½ measure cranberry
    juice
1 measure dry vermouth
3 measures gin
lime slice, to decorate

Put 2–3 ice cubes into a mixing
glass. Pour the grapefruit juice,
cranberry juice, vermouth and
gin over the ice then stir gently.
Put 4–5 fresh ice cubes into a
chilled hurricane glass and strain
the drink over the ice. Decorate
with a lime slice.

Serves 1

Morning Glory Fizz

coolers & fizzers

4–5 ice cubes
1 measure fresh lemon
   juice
½ teaspoon sugar syrup
   (see page 7)
3 measures gin
1 egg white
3 drops pernod
ginger ale

Put the ice cubes into a cocktail shaker. Pour the lemon juice, sugar syrup and gin over the ice. Add the egg white, then the pernod and shake until a frost forms. Strain into a chilled old-fashioned glass, top up with ginger ale and serve with a straw.

Serves 1

Variation

The Morning Glory Fizz can be made with whisky instead of gin.

60

Sydney Fizz

4–5 ice cubes
1 measure fresh lemon
    juice
1 measure fresh orange
    juice
½ teaspoon grenadine
3 measures gin
soda water
orange slice, to decorate

Put the ice cubes into a cocktail shaker. Pour the lemon and orange juices, grenadine and gin over the ice and shake vigorously until a frost forms. Strain into an old-fashioned glass. Top up with soda water, add the orange slice and serve.

Serves 1

Gin Fix

crushed ice cubes
1 tablespoon caster
    sugar
juice of ¼ lemon
1 measure water
2 measures gin
orange and lemon slices,
    to decorate

Fixes are also known as Daisies. They often contain large quantities of fruit or have lavish fruit decorations.

Fill a tall glass two-thirds full with crushed ice. Add the sugar, lemon juice, water and gin and stir well. Decorate the rim of the glass with orange and lemon slices.

Serves 1

Singapore Gin Sling

6–8 ice cubes
juice of ½ lemon
juice of ½ orange
1 measure cherry brandy
3 measures gin
3 drops Angostura bitters
soda water
1 lemon slice, to
    decorate

Put 4–6 ice cubes into a cocktail shaker. Pour the lemon and orange juices, cherry brandy and gin over the ice and add the bitters. Shake the mixture until a frost forms. Put 2 fresh ice cubes into a hurricane glass. Pour the cocktail without straining into the glass and top up with soda water. Decorate with the lemon slice and serve.

Serves 1

Salty Dog

2–3 ice cubes
pinch of salt
1 measure gin
2–2½ measures fresh
    grapefruit juice
orange slice, to decorate

A Salty Dog can also be made with vodka. Sometimes the glass is rimmed with salt, like a Margarita.

Put the ice cubes into an old-fashioned glass. Put the salt on the ice and add the gin and grapefruit juice. Stir gently and serve. Decorate with an orange slice.

Serves 1

Honeydew

1 measure gin
½ measure fresh lemon
    juice
1 dash of pernod
50 g (2 oz) honeydew
    melon, diced
3–4 cracked ice cubes
Champagne

This is the drink to serve at the end of a late Sunday brunch – the combination of honeydew melon and gin makes the perfect transition from breakfast to lunchtime drinks.

Place the gin, lemon juice, pernod and melon in a blender and blend for 30 seconds, then pour into a large wine glass. Top up with Champagne.

Serves 1

John Collins

5–6 ice cubes
1 teaspoon sugar syrup
  (see page 7)
1 measure fresh lemon
  juice
3 measures gin
soda water

to decorate
1 lemon slice
1 mint sprig

The Collins is the tallest of the mixed drinks. It is made with a spirit, lemon juice and water. The John Collins, originally made with Holland's gin, was the first. Now there are also the Mick Collins (Irish whiskey), Pierre Collins (cognac) and the Pedro Collins (made with rum).

Put the ice cubes into a cocktail shaker. Pour in the sugar syrup, lemon juice and gin and shake vigorously until a frost forms. Pour without straining into a Collins glass. Add the lemon and mint and top up with soda water. Stir gently and serve.

Serves 1

Lime Gin Fizz

4–5 ice cubes
2 measures gin
1 measure lime cordial
soda water
lime wedges, to decorate

Put the ice cubes into a tall glass. Pour the gin and the lime cordial over the ice cubes. Top up with soda water, decorate with wedges of lime and serve with straws.

Serves 1

Pink Gin

1–4 dashes Angostura
    bitters
1 measure gin
iced water, to top up

Angostura bitters were developed in the South American town of Angostura in the 19th century. Originally intended for medicinal use, they were put into glasses of gin by the Royal Navy, thus inventing pink gin. Using orange bitters instead of Angostura transforms the drink into a Yellow Gin.

Shake the bitters into a cocktail glass and roll it around until the sides are well coated. Add the gin, then top up with iced water to taste.

Serves 1

High Spirits

Collinson

Alice Springs

Poet's Dream

Moon River

Knockout

Red Kiss

Kiss in the Dark

Earthquake

Burnsides

Woodstock

Stormy Weather

Luigi

Collinson

3 ice cubes, cracked
dash of orange bitters
1 measure gin
½ measure dry vermouth
¼ measure kirsch
piece of lemon rind

to decorate
½ strawberry
lemon slice

Put the ice cubes into a mixing glass, then add the bitters, gin, vermouth and kirsch. Stir well and strain into a cocktail glass. Squeeze the zest from the lemon rind over the surface, and decorate the rim of the glass with the strawberry and lemon.

Serves 1

Alice Springs

4–5 ice cubes
1 measure fresh lemon
    juice
1 measure fresh orange
    juice
½ teaspoon grenadine
3 measures gin
3 drops Angostura bitters
soda water
orange slice, to decorate

Put the ice cubes into a cocktail shaker. Pour in the lemon juice, orange juice, grenadine and gin. Add the bitters and shake until a frost forms. Pour into a tall glass and top up with soda water. Decorate with a slice of orange and serve with straws.

Serves 1

Poet's Dream

4–5 ice cubes
1 measure Bénédictine
1 measure dry vermouth
3 measures gin
1 slice lemon rind

Bénédictine has been made for almost 500 years, originally by the monks of Fécamp Abbey. When mixed with an equal quantity of brandy it is known as a B&B.

Put the ice cubes into a mixing glass. Pour the Bénédictine, vermouth and gin over the ice and stir vigorously, without splashing. Strain into a chilled cocktail glass. Twist the lemon rind over the drink, drop it in and serve.

Serves 1

Moon River

4–5 ice cubes
½ measure dry gin
½ measure apricot brandy
½ measure Cointreau
¼ measure Galliano
¼ measure fresh lemon
    juice
cocktail cherry, to
    decorate

Put some ice cubes into a mixing glass and pour in the gin, apricot brandy, Cointreau, Galliano and lemon juice. Stir then strain the drink into a large chilled cocktail glass. Decorate with the cherry and serve.

Serves 4

Knockout

4–5 ice cubes
1 measure dry vermouth
½ measure white crème
    de menthe
2 measures gin
1 drop pernod
lemon slice, to serve

Crème de menthe is a sweetish mint-flavoured liqueur. It may be green or white, although the flavour remains the same. The white version is used here to blend with the milky colour of the pernod.

Put the ice cubes into a mixing glass. Pour the vermouth, crème de menthe and gin over the ice, stir vigorously, then strain into a chilled old-fashioned glass. Add the pernod and serve with a lemon slice.

Serves 1

Red Kiss

3 ice cubes, cracked
1 measure dry vermouth
½ measure gin
½ measure cherry brandy

to decorate
1 cocktail cherry
spiral of lemon rind

Put the ice cubes into a mixing glass, add the vermouth, gin and cherry brandy and stir well. Strain into a chilled cocktail glass and decorate with the cherry and spiral of lemon.

Serves 1

Kiss in the Dark

4–5 ice cubes
1 measure gin
1 measure cherry brandy
1 teaspoon dry vermouth

Put the ice cubes into a cocktail shaker and pour in the gin, cherry brandy and dry vermouth. Shake then strain into a chilled cocktail glass.

Serves 1

Earthquake

6–8 ice cubes
1 measure gin
1 measure whisky
1 measure pernod

This is an extremely potent concoction. Should an earthquake occur while you are drinking it, commented one 1920s cocktail book, it won't matter.

Put 3–4 ice cubes into a cocktail shaker. Add the gin, whisky and pernod and shake well. Strain into a cocktail glass and add 3–4 fresh ice cubes.

Serves 1

Burnsides

8–10 ice cubes
2 drops Angostura bitters
1 teaspoon cherry brandy
1 measure sweet
    vermouth
2 measures dry
    vermouth
2 measures gin
lemon rind strips, to
    decorate

Put 4–5 ice cubes into a cocktail shaker. Dash the bitters over the ice, add the cherry brandy, sweet and dry vermouths and gin. Shake lightly, then strain into a glass over the remaining ice cubes. Decorate with lemon rind strips.

Serves 1

Woodstock

2–3 ice cubes, crushed
1 measure gin
1 measure dry vermouth
¼ measure Cointreau
1 measure fresh orange
    juice

to decorate
piece of orange rind
orange slice

Put the ice into a cocktail shaker and add the gin, vermouth, Cointreau and orange juice. Shake to mix and strain into a cocktail glass. Squeeze the zest from the orange rind over the surface, and decorate with the orange slice.

Serves 1

Stormy Weather

3 ice cubes, cracked
1½ measures gin
¼ measure Mandarine
    Napoléon liqueur
¼ measure dry vermouth
¼ measure sweet
    vermouth
spiral of orange rind, to
    decorate

Mandarine Napoléon is a French tangerine-flavoured liqueur.

Put the ice cubes into a cocktail shaker and add the gin, Mandarine Napoléon and dry and sweet vermouths. Shake to mix and strain into a chilled cocktail glass. Decorate the rim of the glass with the spiral of orange.

Serves 1

Luigi

4–5 ice cubes
1 measure fresh orange
   juice
1 measure dry vermouth
½ measure Cointreau
1 measure grenadine
2 measures gin
orange slice, to decorate

Put the ice cubes into a mixing glass. Pour the orange juice, vermouth, Cointreau, grenadine and gin over the ice and stir vigorously. Strain into a chilled cocktail glass, decorate with the orange slice and serve.

Serves 1

INDEX

Acknowledgements

Octopus Publishing Group
    Ltd./Neil Mersh 2, 3, 11,
    16, 19, 23, 25, 30, 45, 49,
    53, 55, 59, 61, 67, 70, 72,
    74, 79, 83, 85, 93
/Peter Myers 27, 37, 91
/William Reavell Cover, 5,
    6-7, 8, 13, 15, 20, 28, 33,
    34, 39, 41, 47, 50, 57, 65,
    69, 77, 80, 87, 90
/Simon Smith 42, 62